NOV -- 2011

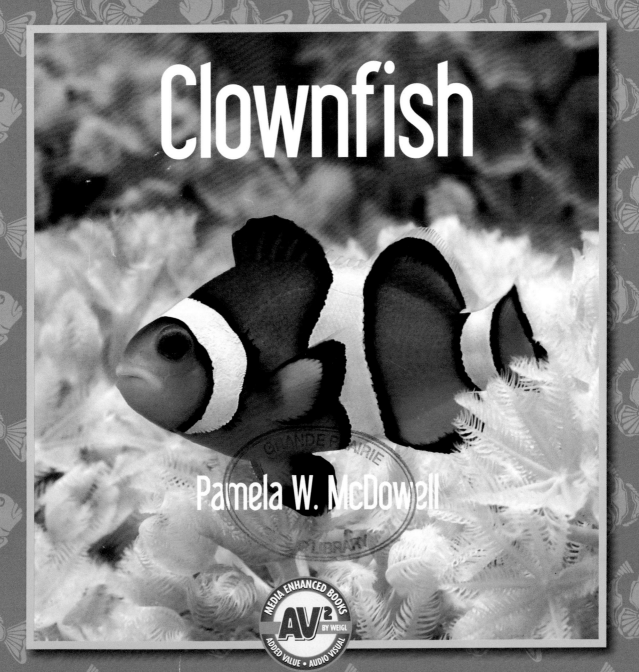

Clownfish

Pamela W. McDowell

AV² BY WEIGL
MEDIA ENHANCED BOOKS
ADDED VALUE · AUDIO VISUAL

www.av2books.com

MEDIA ENHANCED BOOKS
AV²
BY WEIGL™
ADDED VALUE • AUDIO VISUAL

Go to www.av2books.com, and enter this book's unique code.

BOOK CODE

L 5 0 3 8 6 3

AV² by Weigl brings you media enhanced books that support active learning.

AV² provides enriched content that supplements and complements this book. Weigl's AV² books strive to create inspired learning and engage young minds in a total learning experience.

Your AV² Media Enhanced books come alive with...

Audio
Listen to sections of the book read aloud.

Key Words
Study vocabulary, and complete a matching word activity.

Video
Watch informative video clips.

Quizzes
Test your knowledge.

Embedded Weblinks
Gain additional information for research.

Slide Show
View images and captions, and prepare a presentation.

Try This!
Complete activities and hands-on experiments.

... and much, much more!

Published by AV² by Weigl
350 5th Avenue, 59th Floor New York, NY 10118
Website: www.av2books.com   www.weigl.com

Library of Congress Cataloging-in-Publication Data

McDowell, Pamela.
 Clownfish / Pamela McDowell.
    p. cm. -- (Ocean life)
 Includes index.
 ISBN 978-1-61690-692-4 (hardcover : alk. paper) -- ISBN 978-1-61690-696-2 (softcover : alk. paper)
 1. Anemonefishes--Juvenile literature. I. Title.
 QL638.P77M33 2012
 597'.72--dc22
                    2010050415

Printed in the United States of America in North Mankato, Minnesota
1 2 3 4 5 6 7 8 9 0 15 14 13 12 11

052011
WEP37500

Project Coordinator: Aaron Carr
Art Director: Terry Paulhus

Weigl acknowledges Getty Images, Dreamstime, iStockphoto, and Peter Arnold as image suppliers for this title.

CONTENTS

What is a Clownfish?

Have you ever seen a clown with a painted face? There is a type of fish that looks like it is covered in clown paint. It is called a clownfish. Clownfish range in color from yellow to dark reddish-brown. Most clownfish have one or more white stripes.

Clownfish live in the warm waters of the Pacific and Indian Oceans.

Family Stripes

Did you know there are about 28 types of clownfish? Clownfish that are the same type have the same stripes. The common clownfish is usually orange with three white stripes. Thin, black lines often run along the edges of the white stripes. The skunk clownfish has one white stripe running down its back.

How Big is a Clownfish?

Have you ever held a dollar bill? The maroon clownfish can grow up to 6 inches (15 centimeters) long. That is as long as a dollar bill. Most clownfish are about 4 inches (10 cm) long.

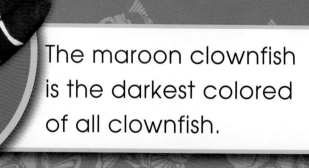

The maroon clownfish is the darkest colored of all clownfish.

A Special House

Did you know the clownfish is also called an anemone fish? A sea anemone is an animal that looks like a flower growing on **coral**. It has hundreds of **tentacles** that sting when touched.

A clownfish makes its home inside an anemone. The clownfish uses the anemone's stingers for protection from **predators**.

Clownfish know which anemone is theirs by its smell.

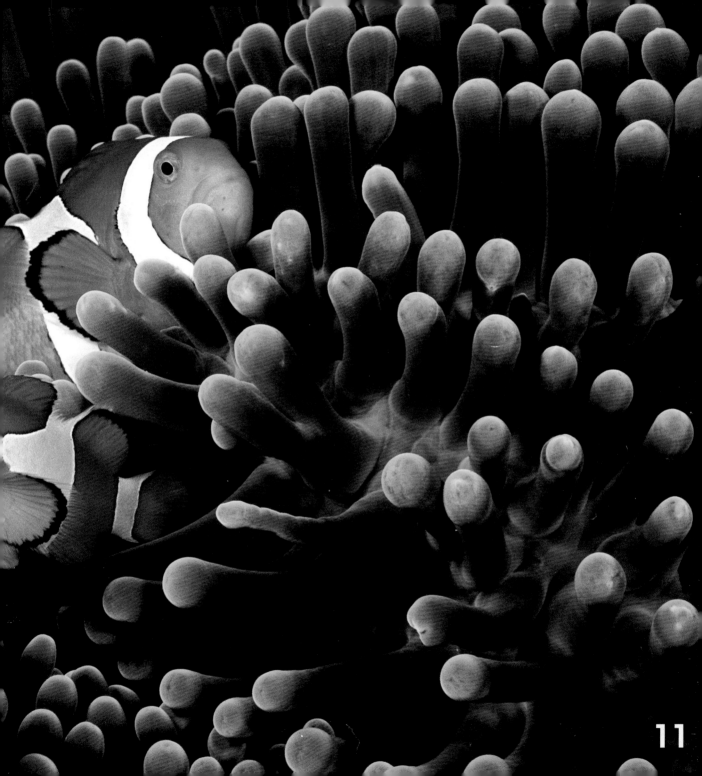

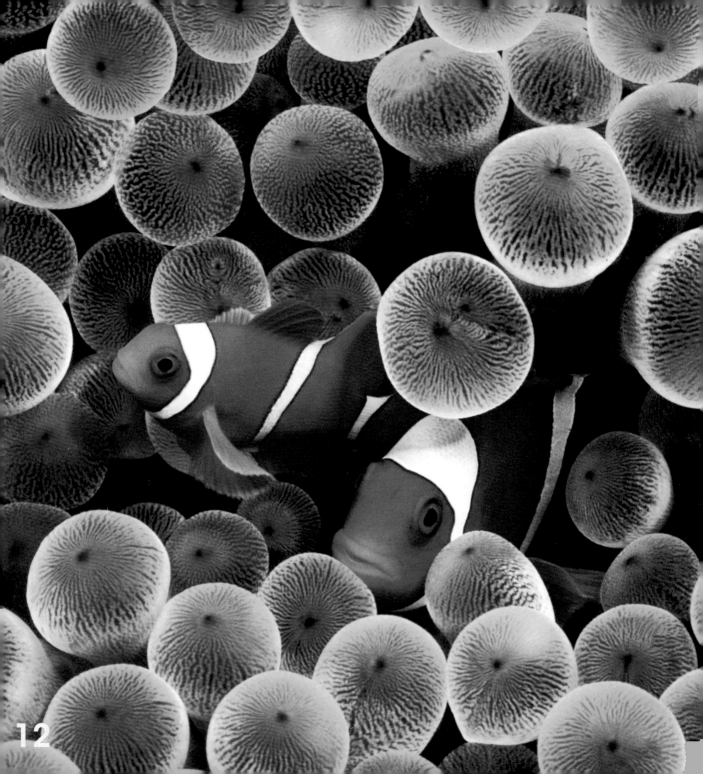

Warning Signs

Why is the clownfish so colorful? The bright colors are a warning to predators. The colors let predators know it is dangerous to eat a clownfish.

Clownfish are coated with special **mucus**. This mucus protects the clownfish from anemone stings. Other fish do not have this mucus. If a predator tries to eat a clownfish, it will get stung and eaten by the anemone.

Friends Forever

Have you ever moved to a new house? A clownfish lives in the same anemone for life. If the anemone moves, the clownfish moves with it.

A clownfish will defend its home. It will attack larger fish that try to eat the anemone. Clownfish even bite divers who swim too close to their home.

Clownfish are not good swimmers. For this reason, they rarely go far from their home.

15

Fishy Food

Can you eat food without chewing it? Clownfish only eat what they can swallow in one bite. Clownfish eat small sea animals and plants. Anemones often leave bits of their food uneaten. Clownfish eat these bits of food. They also eat anemone tentacles that have died.

Super Dads

Did you know clownfish lay thousands of eggs at one time? Clownfish lay their eggs beneath their sea anemone home. Then, the male clownfish guards the eggs until they hatch. All clownfish are born male. The largest fish in a group becomes the only female.

At first, clownfish eggs are bright orange or red. The eggs become clear after a few days.

Clownfish Pets

Have you ever seen clownfish at a pet store? Clownfish can be kept as pets. Caring for a pet clownfish is a challenge.

Clownfish need a large fish tank filled with salt water. The amount of salt in the water must stay the same at all times. Clownfish need to be fed every day. The tank needs to be cleaned every week or two.

Find My Family

Supplies
two sheets of orange construction paper,
scissors, and a black marker

1. With the help of an adult, cut 12 clownfish shapes from the orange construction paper. The shapes should be 4 to 6 inches (10 to 15 cm) long.

2. Draw three matching stripes on 10 of the clownfish using the black marker. This is the family of clownfish.

3. Draw slightly different stripes on the remaining two fish. These are the strangers.

4. Shuffle the clownfish. Then, scatter them on a table. Can you find the 10 that are the same?

5. Reshuffle the clownfish, and scatter them again. Can you find the two strangers? Is it easier to find the strangers or the family?

Glossary

coral: a hard object in the ocean that is made by a small sea animal

mucus: a slimy coating that protects clownfish from sea anemone stings

predators: animals that hunt other animals for food

tentacles: long, slim, flexible parts of an animal

Index

Log on to www.av2books.com

AV² by Weigl brings you media enhanced books that support active learning. Go to www.av2books.com, and enter the special code found on page 2 of this book. You will gain access to enriched and enhanced content that supplements and complements this book. Content includes video, audio, web links, quizzes, a slide show, and activities.

Audio
Listen to sections of the book read aloud.

Video
Watch informative video clips.

Embedded Weblinks
Gain additional information for research.

Try This!
Complete activities and hands-on experiments.

WHAT'S ONLINE?

 Try This!

Gain a better understanding of a clownfish's size with a fun comparison activity.

Identify the benefits of a clownfish's defensive adaptations.

Complete a fun coloring activity.

 Embedded Weblinks

Find out more information on clownfish.

Check out myths and legends about clownfish.

Learn more about a clownfish's diet and nutrition.

Read about an issue facing clownfish.

Video

Watch an introductory video on clownfish.

Watch a video of a clownfish in its natural environment.

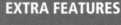 **EXTRA FEATURES**

 Audio
Listen to sections of the book read aloud.

 Key Words
Study vocabulary, and complete a matching word activity.

 Slide Show
View images and captions, and prepare a presentation.

 Quizzes
Test your knowledge.

AV² was built to bridge the gap between print and digital. We encourage you to tell us what you like and what you want to see in the future. Sign up to be an AV² Ambassador at www.av2books.com/ambassador.

Due to the dynamic nature of the Internet, some of the URLs and activities provided as part of AV² by Weigl may have changed or ceased to exist. AV² by Weigl accepts no responsibility for any such changes. All media enhanced books are regularly monitored to update addresses and sites in a timely manner. Contact AV² by Weigl at 1-866-649-3445 or av2books@weigl.com with any questions, comments, or feedback.